May you enjoy great oral health!

Best

ISBN-13: 978-1979261272
ISBN-10: 197926127X

Dedicated to James and Eliana.
Two of the best children and
grandchildren we could ask for.
We love you both with all our hearts
and are so proud of the
people you are becoming.

DENTAL HI JEAN

A STORY ABOUT THE LAND CALLED THE ORAL CAVITY

BY JEAN PETERSON

ILLUSTRATED BY ALANA STROCK

Once upon a time there was a little girl named Jean who liked to visit the land called

"The Oral Cavity"

1

Every day Jean would go into the forest of teeth that were standing in a row like trees.

She would take a piece of string called "Dental Floss" and go in between each tooth, rubbing it gently up against each side of the tooth.

Then she would take a nice soft toothbrush with a pea-sized amount of toothpaste, and brush each tooth in little circles and close to the gum line.

Oh yeah, and Jean never forgot the tongue. The tongue was special because it had cute little taste buds on it.

Jean had a very special brush that she would use to clean all those cute little taste buds on the tongue.

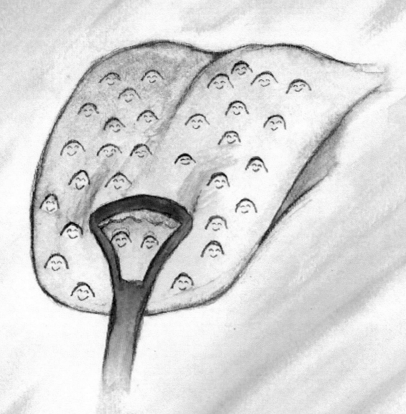

The taste buds preferred the special tongue brush because it did a good job cleaning them.

4

After that she would take some mouth wash to rinse her teeth and swish it all around the land.

Her teeth loved this time
as it made them feel
nice and clean.
It even made them sparkle
when the sun came out.

One day Jean forgot to clean the forest of teeth and the little taste buds on the tongue.

She was so busy with other things that day, she didn't even notice that the teeth were losing their sparkle and the taste buds were being covered up by something sticky.

That something sticky was none other then the evil villain

PLAQUE.

Plaque was an evil villain because he loved to take away the sparkle from the teeth in the forest and make them look ugly.

He would also cover the tongue and taste buds. He could cover them so much that they all looked white and mashed together.

The very next day Jean came to The Oral Cavity and saw the ugliness that the evil villain had caused.

Her teeth looked yellow and her tongue was all white.

Her beautiful forest of teeth even had yucky stuff in between them.

She couldn't see her little
taste buds at all and her poor
teeth were so sad. She felt
terrible and began to cry.

She grabbed her soft toothbrush, floss, and tongue brush and began to get rid of that evil villain.

It was going to take her a little more time then usual because Plaque was rather sticky and harder to get rid of when he became so powerful.

She started with flossing
between her forest of teeth
and then brushed in little
circles all over each tooth.

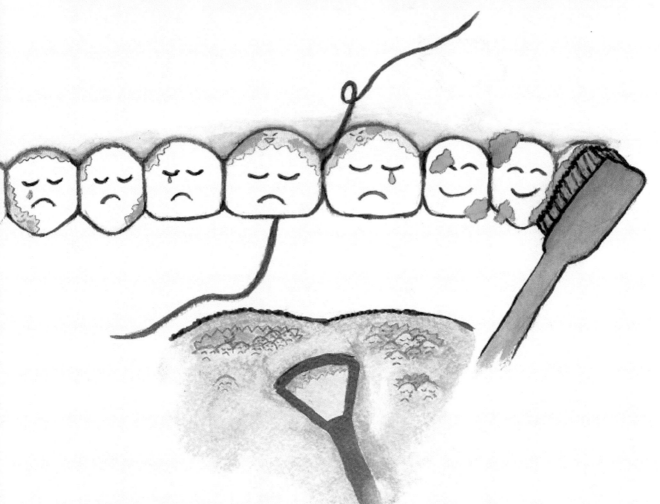

She then gently used the
tongue brush to take Plaque
off of her cute little taste buds.

Then she ran and got a bottle of mouthwash.

She poured a little into a cup and added a little water. Then she swished the mouthwash all around her precious land of The Oral Cavity.

She rinsed them so that they were so clean and shiny that her teeth even sparkled in the sun again.

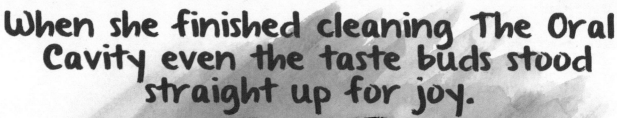

When she finished cleaning The Oral Cavity even the taste buds stood straight up for joy.

When she saw how nice the Oral Cavity looked, Jean promised never to miss a day of brushing, flossing, and rinsing her beautiful land again.

Jean kept her promise and the land called "The Oral Cavity" stayed healthy, clean, and never saw the evil villain Plaque again.

THE END

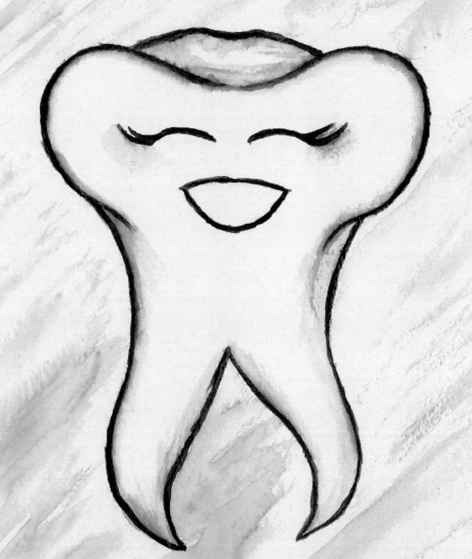

Message From The Author

Oral hygiene care is of the utmost importance. Prevention is the key factor in keeping everyone in good oral health. A simple oral hygiene routine and a six month cleaning can catch issues early and prevent any major oral health issues. Some oral hygiene tips would be the H2O Swish and Swallow Technique which states:

"If you have hydrating drinks, fruit juices, milk, coffee, tea, wine, or any drink that might have sugar (including both natural and artificial sugars) that you would try to drink them in one sitting, then take a big drink of water and swish it all around your mouth (especially around your lower front teeth) then swallow it. This dilutes the sugar to help hamper the incidence of decay."

Swishing with water and chewing a couple of pieces of gum with xylitol after meals helps to hamper the incidence of cavities. Remember to floss, then brush; you can use a tongue brush too. Floss picks that are V shaped fit well in your pocket and are great for travel. As well when you are traveling, within an hour of your evening meal and you are going to have only water, floss and brush your teeth and you will keep your mouth clean until breakfast which will hamper the incidence of cavities.

Hope these tips are helpful!

Made in the USA
Columbia, SC
15 January 2018